Editor
Eric Migliaccio

Managing Editor
Ina Massler Levin, M.A.

Cover Artist
Barb Lorseyedi

Art Manager
Kevin Barnes

Art Director
CJae Froshay

Imaging
Rosa C. See

Publisher
Mary Dupuy Smith, M.S. Ed.

Practice Makes Perfect
Sentence Combining

GRADE 4

D1243796

Author

Ruth Foster, M. Ed.

Teacher Created Resources, Inc.
6421 Industry Way
Westminster, CA 92683
www.teachercreated.com
ISBN: 978-1-4206-8627-2
©2005 Teacher Created Resources, Inc.
Reprinted, 2010
Made in U.S.A.

Table of Contents

The information used in this book comes from the following sources:

Cox, Lynne. *Swimming to Antarctica.* Alfred A. Knopf, 2004.

Erdoes, Richard, and Ortiz, Alfonso. *American Indian Myths and Legends.* Pantheon Books, 1984.

Foster, Ruth. *Take Five Minutes: Fascinating Facts About Geography.* Teacher Created Materials, 2003.

Leokum, Arkady. *Tell Me Why #2.* Grosset & Dunlap, 1986.

Reef, Catherine. *Black Explorers.* Facts on File, Inc., 1996.

Wood, Linda C. *Zoobooks: Zebras.* Wildlife Education, Ltd., 1989.

Wulffson, Don L. *The Kid Who Invented the Popsicle and Other Surprising Stories About Inventions.* Cobblehill Books/Dutton, 1997.

———. *The Kid Who Invented the Trampoline: More Surprising Stories About Inventions.* Dutton Children's Books, 2001.

Introduction

The old adage "practice makes perfect" can really hold true for your child and his or her education. The more practice and exposure your child has with concepts being taught in school, the more success he or she is likely to find. For many parents, knowing how to help their children may be frustrating because practice sources may not be readily available.

It is also difficult to know where to focus your efforts as a parent so that the extra practice your child receives at home supports what he or she is learning in school. This book has been written to help parents and teachers reinforce basic skills with children. *Practice Makes Perfect: Sentence Combining* provides practice with crafting and recognizing well-built sentences. Exercises are provided that allow a child to combine the bits of information found in short sentences. New sentences that are well written and grammatically correct are then built from that information. The exercises in this book can be done sequentially or taken out of order, as needed.

There are two options when it comes to how a child marks what new sentence best combines the short sentences provided: a child can either circle the answers on the exercise pages or use the reproducible fill-in answers sheets found on pages 46 and 47. The practice tests located on pages 42–45 provide a fill-in bubble next to each answer.

Meeting Standards

The standards or objectives that follow will be met or reinforced by completing the practice pages included in this book. These standards and objectives appropriate for the fourth grade and are similar to the ones required by your state and school district:

- The student will demonstrate competence in learning to recognize and to construct clear and grammatically correct simple, compound, and complex sentences.
- The student will demonstrate familiarity with adjectives, adverbs, prepositional phrases, appositives, dependent clauses, and coordinate conjunctions.
- The student will be familiar with different types of writing (fiction and nonfiction).

How to Make the Most of This Book

Here are some useful ideas for making the most of this book:

- Set up a certain time of day to work on these practice pages to establish consistency.
- Keep all practice sessions with your child positive and constructive. If the mood becomes frustrated or tense, set the book aside and look for another time to practice with your child.
- Help beginning readers with instructions.
- If your child needs reading practice, have your child read the exercises out loud. Because the answers repeat all the words in the short sentences, the exercises are a great way for a child to practice reading and improve sight-word vocabulary.
- If your child is having trouble identifying the correct sentence, try reading the answer choices out loud. Often a child can tell that something sounds wrong even if he or she does not visually spot the errors.
- Pay attention to the areas in which your child has the most difficulty. Provide extra guidance and exercises in those areas.

The Yo-Yo

Directions: Read the short sentences. Pick the answer choice that best combines the information in the short sentences. Your answer should be clear and grammatically correct.

1. | Donald Duncan was an American.
   | Donald Duncan went to the Philippines.
   | Donald Duncan went in the 1920s.

   a. Donald Duncan was an American who went to the Philippines in the 1920s.

   b. Donald Duncan, an American, went in the 1920s.

   c. In the 1920s, Donald Duncan went to the Philippines because he was an American.

   d. Donald Duncan in the 1920s went to the Philippines and was an American.

2. | Duncan saw some people in the Philippines.
   | The people were hunting.
   | The people used a weapon.
   | The weapon looked funny.

   a. Duncan saw some funny-looking people hunting with a weapon in the Philippines.

   b. Some people in the Philippines used a funny weapon that Duncan saw.

   c. Duncan saw some people hunting with a funny-looking weapon in the Philippines.

   d. The people Duncan saw in the Philippines were hunting and using a funny weapon.

3. | The weapon was large.
   | The weapon was round.
   | The weapon was a disk.
   | The weapon was made out of wood.
   | The weapon was made out of stone.

   a. The weapon was a large, round disk made out of wood or made out of stone.

   b. The weapon was large and round and a disk made out of wood or stone.

   c. The disk was large and round and a weapon made out of wood or made out of stone.

   d. The weapon was a large, round disk made out of wood or stone.

The Yo-Yo (cont.)

4.
> Rope was wrapped around the disk.
>
> Hunters threw the disk.
>
> Hunters threw at animals.

   a. Rope was wrapped around the disk, and hunters threw animals at it.

   b. Hunters wrapped rope around the disk and threw it at animals.

   c. Hunters wrapped the disk and threw the rope around the animals.

   d. Rope was wrapped around the disk and thrown at animals by hunters.

5.
> The rope got tangled.
>
> It got tangled around legs.
>
> The legs were on animals.
>
> The animals were trapped.

   a. Animals got trapped when the animals got the rope and their legs were tangled.

   b. Animals were trapped when the rope got tangled around their legs.

   c. Animals' legs got tangled in the rope and trapped in the legs.

   d. Animals got their legs trapped when the rope got tangled in them.

6.
> The weapon gave Duncan an idea.
>
> The idea was for a toy.
>
> The toy was small.
>
> The toy is known today.
>
> It is called a yo-yo.

   a. Duncan made a toy weapon from an idea known today as the yo-yo.

   b. Duncan got a small idea for a toy today called a yo-yo.

   c. The weapon gave Duncan an idea for a small toy known today as the yo-yo.

   d. Known today as the yo-yo, Duncan got an idea for a weapon.

Fun Fact! Did you know that "yo-yo" means "come-come" in the Philippines hunters' language?

Should We Tell?

Directions: Read the short sentences. Pick the answer choice that best combines the information in the short sentences. Your answer should be clear and grammatically correct.

1.
> Abdul and I had to make a thing.
>
> Abdul is my best friend.
>
> The thing had to be new.
>
> The thing had to taste good.

   a. I and Abdul, my best friend, had to make a thing new and good-tasting.

   b. Abdul, my best friend, and I had to make a new, good-tasting thing.

   c. I had to make a thing new and taste good, and Abdul is my best friend.

   d. The thing, new and good-tasting, Abdul, my friend, and I had to make.

2.
> We made treats.
>
> The treats were healthy.
>
> The treats were for dogs.
>
> The treats were to sell at the fair.
>
> The fair was our school fair.

   a. We made treats for healthy dogs to sell at our school fair.

   b. At our school fair, we made healthy dog treats.

   c. We made treats for healthy dogs at our school fair.

   d. We made healthy dog treats to sell at our school fair.

3.
> We rolled eggs.
>
> We rolled cheese.
>
> The cheese was in bits.
>
> We rolled food.
>
> The food was for dogs.
>
> The eggs, cheese, and food were together.
>
> Then we cut out shapes.

   a. We rolled eggs, bits of cheese, and dog food together, and then we cut out shapes.

   b. Cutting out shapes, we rolled eggs, bits of cheese, and dog food together then.

   c. We rolled eggs and bits of cheese together, and then dog food we cut into shapes.

   d. The eggs, dog food, and cheese we rolled together was in bits, and then we cut out shapes.

Should We Tell? *(cont.)*

4.
> We left them to cool.
>
> We left them on the table.
>
> The table was in the kitchen.
>
> We left them after baking the treats.
>
> The treats were healthy.

   a. After baking the healthy treats, we left them on the kitchen table to cool.

   b. The treats that were healthy and cool we left on the kitchen table after baking.

   c. Leaving them on the kitchen table to cool after, we baked the healthy treats.

   d. To cool the healthy treats, on the kitchen table, we left them.

5.
> Jess came in.
>
> Jess was Abdul's brother.
>
> Abdul was older than Jess.
>
> Jess ate cookies.
>
> The eating was secret.
>
> The number of cookies he ate was two.

   a. Abdul's brother Jess secretly ate two older cookies and came in.

   b. Jess, Abdul's younger brother, came in and secretly ate two cookies.

   c. Eating two cookies with secrecy, Jess came in with Abdul's older brother.

   d. Jess, the younger brother of Abdul, ate two cookies and came in secretly.

6.
> He asked, "What makes them taste so good?"
>
> When he asked, he reached for more.

   a. "What makes them taste so good?" he reached for more, asking.

   b. When he asked, "What makes them taste so good?" reaching for more.

   c. "What makes them taste so good?" he asked, reaching for more.

   d. Reaching, he asked for more, "What makes them taste so good?"

Fun Fact! Did you know that we taste with our taste buds that are located on our tongues? We cannot taste with our feet, like some flies and butterflies!

Swimming in Antarctica

Directions: Read the short sentences. Pick the answer choice that best combines the information in the short sentences. Your answer should be clear and grammatically correct.

1.
> Lynne Cox is a swimmer.
>
> Cox swims long distances.
>
> Cox swam in Antarctica.
>
> The waters of Antarctica are freezing.

   a. Lynne Cox is a swimmer who swims long distances and swam in the freezing waters of Antarctica.

   b. Lynne Cox, a long-distance swimmer, swam in the freezing waters of Antarctica.

   c. A long-distance swimmer, Lynne Cox swam, freezing in Antarctica waters.

   d. Lynne Cox, a long-distance swimmer, swam in Antarctica, and the waters are freezing.

2.
> The water was only 32 degrees.
>
> She still swam.
>
> She didn't wear a wet suit.

   a. The water was only 32 degrees, and she still swam, and she didn't wear a wet suit.

   b. She didn't wear when she swam a wet suit, and the water was only 32 degrees.

   c. She didn't wear a wet suit, still swam, but the water was only 32 degrees.

   d. The water was only 32 degrees, but still she swam without a wet suit.

3.
> Cox was surrounded at one point.
>
> Cox was surrounded during her swim.
>
> Her swim was for one mile.
>
> Penguins surrounded Cox.
>
> The penguins were chinstraps.

   a. Cox was surrounded at one point during her swim that was for one mile by chinstrap penguins.

   b. During her one-mile swim, penguins that were chinstraps at one point surrounded Cox.

   c. At one point during her one-mile swim, chinstrap penguins surrounded Cox.

   d. At one point during her one-mile swim, Cox was surrounded by penguins that were chinstraps.

Swimming in Antarctica (cont.)

4.

> The penguins were a sign.
>
> The sign was good.
>
> The sign meant that there were not any killer whales in the area.
>
> The sign meant that there were not any leopard seals in the area.

    a. The penguins were a good sign because it meant that there weren't any killer whales or leopard seals in the area.

    b. The penguins were a sign that was good because it meant that there weren't any killer whales or leopard seals in the area.

    c. The good penguins in the area signed that there weren't any killer whales or leopard seals.

    d. The sign of the area penguins meant that there weren't any good killer whales or leopard seals.

5.

> When Cox stopped something happened.
>
> Cox could not control something.
>
> Cox could not control her shaking.

    a. When Cox stopped, she couldn't control her shaking.

    b. Cox stopped when something happened, and she couldn't control her shaking.

    c. When she could not control her shaking, Cox stopped.

    d. Cox stopped when she could not control what happened or her shaking.

6.

> Cox wore clothes to warm up.
>
> The clothes were special.
>
> The clothes had packs sewn into them.
>
> The packs were chemical.
>
> The chemicals emitted heat.

    a. Cox wore clothes that were special to warm up, and the clothes had heat-emitting chemical packs sewn into them.

    b. To warm up, Cox wore special clothes that had packs that were chemical and emitted heat sewn into them.

    c. To warm up, Cox wore special clothes that had heat-emitting chemical packs sewn into them.

    d. The chemical packs that emitted heat sewn into Cox's clothing to warm her up made them special.

Fun Fact! Did you know that Cox was the first person in the world to swim a mile in Antarctica, as well as across the Bering Strait and the Strait of Magellan?

My Dog Hercules

Directions: Read the short sentences. Pick the answer choice that best combines the information in the short sentences. Your answer should be clear and grammatically correct.

1.
> Hercules is my dog.
>
> Hercules is big.
>
> Hercules is black.
>
> Hercules is scary to look at.

   a. Hercules is my dog, and big and black and scary-looking he is.

   b. My dog Hercules is big, black, and scary-looking.

   c. My dog Hercules is black, and he is big, and he is scary to look at.

   d. My scary-looking Hercules is big and is black and is a dog.

2.
> My dog is named after Hercules.
>
> Hercules is from a Greek myth.
>
> Hercules is a hero.

   a. My dog is named after Hercules from the Greek hero myth.

   b. My dog is named after the mythological hero Hercules, and Hercules is Greek.

   c. Hercules is a hero from a Greek myth and that is who my dog is named after.

   d. My dog is named after Hercules, the mythological Greek hero.

3.
> Hercules is brave in the myth.
>
> I thought my dog was brave like Hercules.

   a. In the myth, Hercules is brave, and I thought my dog was brave, to.

   b. In the myth, Hercules is brave, and I thought my dog was brave, too.

   c. Hercules is brave, and I thought my dog was brave in the myth, too.

   d. Hercules is brave in the myth, and I thought my dog was brave like Hercules two.

My Dog Hercules (cont.)

4. | Hercules would bark wildly.
Hercules would scare our kittens.
We had three kittens.
The kittens were little.
The kittens would go up a tree.

a. Hercules, barking wildly, would scare our three little kittens up a tree.

b. Hercules would scare our three kittens barking wildly up a little tree.

c. Hercules would bark wildly and would scare our three kittens that were little up a tree.

d. Our three little kittens would scare up a tree when Hercules would bark wildly.

5. | A storm blew in.
The storm was big.
It came one night.
The power went out.

a. A storm that was big blew in one night, and the power went out.

b. One night a big storm went in, and the power blew out.

c. One night a big storm blew in, and the power went out.

d. The power went out one big night when the storm blew in.

6. | It was dark.
Hercules trembled in fear.
There were three kittens.
The kittens were little.
The kittens played.
They played merrily.

a. Trembling in fear, Hercules played merrily with the three little kittens in the dark.

b. It was dark, and Hercules trembled in fear while the little kittens three merrily played.

c. While they played merrily, Hercules trembled in fear with the three little kittens.

d. Hercules trembled in fear while the three little kittens played merrily in the dark.

Fun fact! Did you know that being brave has nothing to do with size or how one looks?

Where in the World?

Directions: Read the short sentences. Pick the answer choice that best combines the information in the short sentences. Your answer should be clear and grammatically correct.

1.
> A city lies.
>
> The city is ancient.
>
> The city is Incan.
>
> The city lies in ruins.
>
> The city is in the Andes Mountains.
>
> The city is high.

   a. In the ancient Andes Mountains ruins lies a high Incan city.

   b. In the ruins of the high Andes Mountains lies an ancient Incan city.

   c. The Incan city lies in the high Andes Mountains ancient ruins.

   d. The ruins of an ancient Incan city lie high in the Andes Mountains.

2.
> Stones were placed.
>
> The placement was careful.
>
> Not even a sheet of paper could fit between them.
>
> The sheets were thin.

   a. Not even a thin sheet of paper could fit between the carefully placed stones.

   b. Not even a thin sheet of paper could carefully fit between the placed stones.

   c. With careful placement, not even a sheet of paper could fit between the stones.

   d. Stones were placed careful with thin sheets that could not even fit between.

3.
> Incan doctors were advanced.
>
> The advancement was high.
>
> The doctors know how to perform surgery.
>
> The surgery was on the brain.
>
> The doctors knew how to fill teeth.

   a. Knowing how to perform brain surgery and fill teeth, highly advanced Incan doctors.

   b. Highly advanced Incan doctors knew how to perform brain surgery and fill teeth.

   c. Incan doctors knew how to fill teeth and to perform highly advanced brain surgery.

   d. Brain surgery highly advanced Incan doctors on how to fill teeth.

Where in the World? *(cont.)*

4. | People ate potatoes.
The people were in the city.
The potatoes are food.
The food was cultivated in the Andes.
It was cultivated first.

   a. Cultivated first in the Andes, people in the city ate food potatoes.

   b. A food first cultivated in the Andes, the people in the city ate potatoes.

   c. The people in the city ate potatoes, a food first cultivated in the Andes.

   d. In the city, a food first cultivated in the Andes was eaten by people.

5. | Llamas were used for food.
Llamas were used for transport.
Llamas are animals.
The animals are like camels.

   a. Llamas were used for food and camel-like transport.

   b. Used for food and used for transport were camel-like llama animals.

   c. Animals, camel-like llamas, were food and used for transport.

   d. Llamas, camel-like animals, were used for food and transport.

6. | Peru has borders.
One border is Brazil.
One border is Chile.
Peru lies on the ocean.
The ocean is the Pacific.

   a. Bordering Brazil and Chile, Peru lies on the Pacific Ocean.

   b. Bordering Peru is Brazil and Chile where it lies on the Pacific Ocean.

   c. Peru borders Brazil and Chile where it lies on the Pacific Ocean.

   d. Lying on the ocean of the Pacific is Peru, bordering Brazil and Chile.

Fun Fact! **Did you know that people in Peru learned long ago how to freeze-dry potatoes? The freeze-dried potatoes are good for about four years.**

Riddles

Directions: Read the short sentences. Pick the answer choice that best combines the information in the short sentences. Your answer should be clear and grammatically correct.

1.
> What is it?
>
> It always runs.
>
> It never walks.
>
> It has a bed.
>
> It never sleeps.

   a. Always runs, never walks, has a bed, never sleeps, is it what?

   b. It always runs, it never walks, it has a bed, and it never sleeps, and what is it?

   c. Always running and never sleeping, and it has a bed, what never walks?

   d. What is it that always runs, never walks, has a bed, and never sleeps?

2.
> A river runs.
>
> A river has a bed.
>
> A river never sleeps!

   a. A river never runs, and a river has a bed, and a river sleeps!

   b. Having a bed, a river sleeps and never runs!

   c. Never sleeping, a river runs and has a bed!

   d. A river runs and has a bed, but it never sleeps!

3.
> What is it?
>
> It has legs.
>
> The number of legs is four.
>
> It cannot walk.
>
> It can stand.

   a. It has four legs, and it cannot walk, but it can stand, and is it what?

   b. What is it that has four legs and can stand but cannot walk?

   c. What is it that cannot walk but can stand, and four is the number of legs?

   d. With four the leg number, it can stand, but it cannot walk, and what is it?

Riddles *(cont.)*

4. | A table cannot walk.
A table is large or small.
A table has legs.

   a. A table, large or small, has legs, but a table cannot walk.

   b. With large or small legs, a table cannot walk.

   c. A large or small table has legs, but the legs cannot walk.

   d. A table, with legs, cannot walk, large or small.

5. | Ducks stand.
Pigs stand.
People stand.
The standing is under an umbrella.
The number of ducks is 16.
The number of pigs is five.
The number of people is two.
How can they all not get wet when standing?

   a. How can they all not get wet when standing, the 16 ducks, five pigs, and two people under an umbrella?

   b. The ducks, numbering 16, the pigs, numbering five, and the people, numbering two, stand under an umbrella, and how can they all not get wet?

   c. How can 16 ducks, five pigs, and two people stand under an umbrella and not get wet?

   d. How can they all not get wet when standing under an umbrella, the 16 ducks, the five pigs, and the two people?

6. | The ducks stood.
The pigs stood.
The people stood.
The standing was under the umbrella.
The standing was when it wasn't raining!

   a. The ducks, pigs, and people stood under the umbrella when it wasn't raining!

   b. The ducks and the pigs and the people stood under the umbrella when it wasn't raining!

   c. When it wasn't raining, the standing was under the umbrella by the ducks, pigs, and people.

   d. Standing under the umbrella, ducks, pigs, and people, when it wasn't raining.

Fun Fact! Did you know that the longest word in the world is "smiles"? There is a "mile" between each "s"!

The Zebra

Directions: Read the short sentences. Pick the answer choice that best combines the information in the short sentences. Your answer should be clear and grammatically correct.

1.
> A zebra baby is a foal.
>
> A foal has legs.
>
> The legs are extremely long.

    a. A zebra baby is a foal that is born with long legs extremely.

    b. A zebra baby is called a foal, and it has extremely long foal legs when it is born.

    c. When it is born, a foal that is a baby zebra has extremely long legs.

    d. A zebra baby, or foal, is born with extremely long legs.

2.
> The foal can run with its legs.
>
> The foal can keep up with its legs.
>
> The legs are almost adult-sized.
>
> The foal can keep up with the herd within an hour.
>
> The hour is after its birth.

    a. With its almost adult-sized legs, the foal can run and keep up with the herd within an hour after its birth.

    b. Within an hour after its birth, the foal's legs can almost keep up and run with the adult-sized herd.

    c. The foal can keep up with the herd within an hour after its birth on its almost adult-sized legs it can run with and keep up with.

    d. With its legs that are almost adult-sized, within an hour of its birth, the foal can run with the herd and keep up with the herd.

3.
> Zebras roll.
>
> They roll in the mud.
>
> They roll in the dust.
>
> They roll to take a bath.

    a. Zebras roll in the mud, or zebras roll in the dust to take a bath.

    b. Zebras roll to take a mud bath in the dust.

    c. In the mud or the dust zebras roll to take a bath.

    d. To take a bath, zebras roll in the mud or dust.

The Zebra (cont.)

4.
> Zebras shake when the mud dries.
>
> Zebras shake the mud off.
>
> Loose hair shakes off with the mud.
>
> Flakes of skin shake off with the mud.
>
> The skin is dry.

   a. Zebras shake when the mud dries so that the mud shakes off, along with loose hairs and shaking dry flakes of skin.

   b. When the mud dries, zebras shake it off, along with loose hair and flakes of dry skin.

   c. Flakes of dry skin and loose hairs are shaken off along with the mud by the zebra when it has dried.

   d. Zebras shake it off, drying the mud, loose hair, and flakes of skin.

5.
> The film is left on the skin.
>
> The film is of dust.
>
> The film acts as a shield.
>
> The shield is against heat.
>
> The shield is against wind.
>
> The shield is against insects.

   a. The film left on the skin is of dust and acts as a shield against heat, and wind and insects.

   b. A shield against heat, wind, and insects, is the film of dust left on the skin.

   c. The film of dust left on the skin acts as a shield against heat, wind, and insects.

   d. Left on the skin, the dust of film acts as a heat, wind, and insect shield.

6.
> Some birds help the zebras stay clean.
>
> They help by eating pests.
>
> The pests are little.
>
> The pests burrow in the zebras' skin.

   a. The little pests that burrow in the zebras' skin are helped by some birds eating them.

   b. Some birds that eat the little pests that burrow in the zebras' skin help stay clean.

   c. Some birds help the zebras stay clean by eating the tiny pests that burrow in the zebras' skin.

   d. Burrowing in the zebras' skin, the little pests are eaten by some clean birds.

Fun Fact! Did you know that no two zebras are exactly alike? Just as we have our own fingerprints, zebras have their own stripe patterns.

The Scary Ride

Directions: Read the short sentences. Pick the answer choice that best combines the information in the short sentences. Your answer should be clear and grammatically correct.

1. | The city park has a ride.
   One ride is through a tunnel.
   The tunnel is dark.
   The tunnel is scary.

   a. One dark, scary, ride is through city park and in a tunnel.
   b. One ride in the city park is through a dark, scary tunnel.
   c. Through a dark, scary tunnel is the one city park ride.
   d. One ride, scary and dark, is through a city tunnel in the park.

2. | My friends would go on the ride.
   Jake was my friend.
   Jon was my friend.
   Sarah was my friend.
   I was too scared.

   a. My friends would go on the ride, Jake, Jon, and Sarah, but I was too scared.
   b. My friends Jake, Jon, and Sarah would go on the ride, but I was too scared.
   c. I was scared, but my friends would go on the ride, Jake, Jon, and Sarah too.
   d. My friends, Jake, Jon, and Sarah, but I was too scared, would go on the ride.

3. | The ride was set up as it were a mine.
   The mine was old.
   The ride was full of miners.
   The ride was full of bats.
   The miners and bats were life-like.

   a. Set up as if it were an old mine, the ride was filled with life-like miners and bats.
   b. Set up like a life-like mine, the ride was filled with old miners and bats.
   c. Filled with life-like miners and bats, the old ride was set up as it were a mine.
   d. Filled with miners and life-like bats, the ride was set up as an old mine.

The Scary Ride (cont.)

4.
> The bats brushed your shoulders.
>
> The bats were soft.
>
> The bats hung from strings.
>
> The strings were plastic.

a. The bats brushed your shoulders softly and hung from plastic strings.

b. The soft bats, hanging from plastic strings, brushed your shoulders.

c. Hanging from plastic strings, your shoulders and the soft bats brushed.

d. Brushing your shoulders, the bats hanging from soft plastic strings were.

5.
> I went on the ride.
>
> The ride was silly.
>
> I went because I did not want to be teased.
>
> The teasing was about being afraid.

a. Not wanting to be teased about being afraid, I went on the silly ride.

b. I went on the ride that was silly, not wanting to be teased about being afraid.

c. Being afraid, I went on the silly ride not to be teased.

d. Not wanting to be teased, I went on the silly ride because I was afraid.

6.
> I came out smiling.
>
> The smiling was brave.
>
> The truth is that I had my eyes closed in the tunnel!
>
> The closing was tight.
>
> The tunnel was dark.

a. Smiling bravely, the truth is that I had my eyes tightly closed in the dark tunnel!

b. My eyes tightly closed in the dark tunnel, the truth is that I came out smiling bravely!

c. I came out smiling bravely, but the truth is that I had my eyes tightly closed in the dark tunnel!

d. I, smiling bravely, the truth is, had my tightly closed eyes in the dark tunnel!

Fun Fact! Did you know that some people find roller coasters to be the scariest type of ride?

Albert José Jones

Directions: Read the short sentences. Pick the answer choice that best combines the information in the short sentences. Your answer should be clear and grammatically correct.

1.

> Dr. Albert José Jones scuba dives.
>
> He is a marine biologist.
>
> The diving is in waters.
>
> The waters are all over the world.

    a. A marine biologist scuba diving all over the world in waters is Dr. Albert José Jones.

    b. Dr. Albert José Jones, a marine biologist, scuba dives in waters all over the world.

    c. All over the water in waters a marine biologist Dr. Albert José Jones scuba dives.

    d. Dr. Albert José Jones scuba dives, and he is a marine biologist, and he dives in all over the world waters.

2.

> Jones taught himself to swim.
>
> He was on land.
>
> The land was dry.
>
> He used a bench.
>
> He used a bucket of water.

    a. Using a bench on dry land and a bucket of water, himself taught Jones to swim.

    b. Jones taught himself to swim, and he was on dry land, and he used a bench, and he used a bucket of water.

    c. Jones taught himself to swim on dry land using a bench and a bucket of water.

    d. Swimming on land that was dry, Jones, using a bench and bucket of water, taught himself.

3.

> Jones filled the bucket with water.
>
> Jones put it on the floor.
>
> Jones put it at the end of the bench.

    a. Jones filled the bucket with water, and Jones put it on the floor, and Jones put it at the end of the bench.

    b. Putting it on the floor and at the end of the bench, Jones filled with water the bucket.

    c. Jones filled the bucket with water, and he put it on the floor at the end of the bench.

    d. Jones put the bucket Jones filled with water at the end of the bench on the floor.

Albert José Jones *(cont.)*

4.
> He lay facedown on the bench.
>
> He kicked his feet.
>
> He stroked the air.
>
> The stroking was with his arms.

   a. Lying, kicking facedown, his arms stroked the air on the bench.

   b. Stroking and kicking air and feet, he lay facedown on the bench.

   c. He, on the bench stroking with his arms and kicking, lay facedown in air.

   d. Lying facedown on the bench, he kicked his feet and stroked the air with his arms.

5.
> Jones dunked his head.
>
> The dunking was in and out of the bucket.
>
> Jones matched the rhythm of his strokes.

   a. Jones, matching the rhythm of his strokes, dunked his head in and out of the bucket.

   b. Dunking his head in and out, Jones dunked and matched the bucket stroke rhythm.

   c. The rhythm of his strokes matching the in and out dunking, Jones dunked the bucket.

   d. His strokes in and out of the bucket matching, Jones matched the rhythm.

6.
> Jones would turn every time.
>
> Jones would breathe every time.
>
> The time was when he lifted his head out of the water.

   a. Jones would turn every time, and Jones would breathe every time he lifted his head out of the water.

   b. Every time he turned and breathed out of the water, Jones would lift his head.

   c. Jones would turn and breathe every time, and the time was when he lifted his head out of the water.

   d. Jones would turn and breathe every time he lifted his head out of the water.

Fun Fact! Did you know that in 1993 Jones and other National Association of Black Scuba Diver members laid a plaque at the site of a sunken slave ship? The slave shipwreck was in the Gulf of Mexico.

The Wish

Directions: Read the short sentences. Pick the answer choice that best combines the information in the short sentences. Your answer should be clear and grammatically correct.

1.
> One day Lex found a lamp.
>
> The lamp was old.
>
> The day was in the spring.

    a. One day in the spring, Lex found a lamp that was old.

    b. An old lamp was found by Lex one spring day.

    c. One spring day, Lex found an old lamp.

    d. Lex was one spring day finding an old lamp.

2.
> Lex rubbed it with his hands.
>
> The rubbing cleaned it.
>
> Lex hoped the lamp was magic.

    a. Lex hoped the lamp was magic, and Lex rubbed it with his cleaning hands

    b. Lex, hoping the lamp was magic, rubbed it clean with his hands.

    c. Lex rubbed it with his hands, and the rubbing cleaned it, and Lex hoped the lamp was magic.

    d. Rubbing and hoping the lamp was magic, Lex cleaned it with his hands.

3.
> A genie popped out.
>
> The popping was sudden.
>
> The genie was yellow.
>
> The genie was wearing pants.
>
> The pants were brightly-striped.

    a. Suddenly wearing brightly-striped pants, a yellow genie popped out.

    b. Popping suddenly out, the genie that was yellow wore brightly-striped pants.

    c. Wearing brightly-striped yellow pants, popped out suddenly a genie.

    d. Suddenly, a yellow genie wearing brightly-striped pants popped out.

The Wish (cont.)

4. | The genie smiled.

The genie said, "You may have a wish."

The genie nodded at Lex.

   a. Nodding at Lex, the genie smiled and said, "You may have a wish."

   b. The genie smiled, and the genie said, "You may have a wish," and the genie nodded at Lex.

   c. "You may have a wish," the genie nodded at Lex and smiled and said.

   d. Smiling and nodding at Lex, "You may have a wish," said the genie.

5. | Lex wished to fly.

The genie told Lex the wish could be granted.

The granting could be easy.

The genie was kind.

   a. Wishing he could fly, the kind genie told Lex the wish could be granted easy.

   b. The genie that was kind told Lex that granting the wish to fly could be easy.

   c. Lex wished to fly, and the kind genie told him the wish could be easily granted.

   d. Lex wished to fly, and the genie told Lex the wish could be granted easily, and the genie was kind.

6. | Lex knew the wish came true.

The wish came not the way he expected!

Lex knew when his dad surprised him.

The surprising was with plane tickets.

The tickets were to Mexico.

   a. When his dad surprised him, Lex knew the wish came true—but not the way with plane tickets to Mexico he expected!

   b. When his dad surprised him with plane tickets to Mexico, Lex knew the wish came true—but not the way he expected!

   c. With surprising plane tickets to Mexico, Lex's dad knew the wish came true—but not the way he expected!

   d. Lex, surprised by his dad with plane tickets—but knew the Mexico wish, not expected, came true!

Fun Fact! Did you know that the first time an engine-powered machine ever elevated itself off the ground and flew was on December 17, 1903? The machine was Orville and Wilbur Wright's plane.

The Magic School Bus

Directions: Read the short sentences. Pick the answer choice that best combines the information in the short sentences. Your answer should be clear and grammatically correct.

1.
> The Magic School Bus is a book.
>
> Joanna Cole wrote *The Magic School Bus.*
>
> The Magic School Bus is good to read.

   a. *The Magic School Bus* is a good written book that Joanna Cole reads.

   b. A good book to read is written by Joanna Cole, *The Magic School Bus.*

   c. *The Magic School Bus*, written by Joanna Cole, is a good book to read.

   d. Joanna Cole wrote a book, *The Magic School Bus*, good to read,

2.
> Ms. Frizzle is a teacher.
>
> Ms. Frizzle is strange.
>
> Ms. Frizzle takes her class on field trips.
>
> The field trips are even stranger.

   a. A strange teacher, Ms. Frizzle takes field trips with her even stranger class.

   b. The field trips Ms. Frizzle, a strange teacher, takes are even stranger than her class.

   c. Ms. Frizzle is a strange teacher who takes her class on even stranger field trips.

   d. The field trips are even stranger than strange Ms. Frizzle, a teacher with a class.

3.
> Something happens when Ms. Frizzle drives the bus.
>
> The bus becomes magic.
>
> The bus is old.
>
> The bus is yellow.
>
> The bus is a school bus.

   a. When Ms. Frizzle drives, the old, yellow school bus becomes magic.

   b. When old Ms. Frizzle drives, the yellow school bus becomes magic.

   c. The old, yellow bus becomes magic when Ms. Frizzle drives it to school.

   d. The school bus, old and yellow, becomes magic when Ms. Frizzle drives the bus.

The Magic School Bus (cont.)

4.
> The bus can fly.
>
> The bus can shrink.
>
> The bus takes the class into space.
>
> The bus takes the class into the center of the Earth.

a. Flying and shrinking, the class takes the bus into space and the Earth's center.

b. The bus can fly and shrink, and it takes the class into space and the Earth's center.

c. The bus can fly and shrink, but it takes the class into the Earth's center space.

d. The center of the Earth and into space is where the shrinking and flying bus takes the class.

5.
> The book has pictures.
>
> The pictures are fun.
>
> The pictures are of clothes.
>
> The clothes are Ms. Frizzle's.
>
> The clothes are very odd.

a. The book has pictures that are fun, as Ms. Frizzle's clothes are very odd.

b. Ms. Frizzle's clothes are very odd, as the book's pictures are fun.

c. The clothes, very odd and Ms. Frizzle's, are fun book pictures.

d. The book's pictures are fun, as Ms. Frizzle's clothes are very odd.

6.
> Sometimes Ms. Frizzle's shoes look like something.
>
> They look like mouths.
>
> The mouths are human.
>
> They look like planets.
>
> They look like plants.
>
> The plants eat flesh!

a. Ms. Frizzle's shoes, human mouths, planets, or flesh-eating plants, look like something.

b. Sometimes Ms. Frizzle's shoes look like human mouths, planets, or flesh-eating plants!

c. Ms. Frizzles sometimes has shoes that look like mouths, planets, or human flesh-eating plants!

d. Looking like human mouths, planets, or plants that eat flesh, are Ms. Frizzle's shoes sometimes!

Fun Fact! Did you know that sometimes a fun way to learn true science facts is by reading fiction (or made-up) books?

The Player

Directions: Read the short sentences. Pick the answer choice that best combines the information in the short sentences. Your answer should be clear and grammatically correct.

1.
   > The player runs.
   >
   > The player twists.
   >
   > The player leaps.
   >
   > The player plays basketball.
   >
   > The player moved down the court.
   >
   > The court is wooden.

   a. The player who played basketball moved down the running, twisting, leaping, court.

   b. The player, moving, twisting, leaping, running down the wooden basketball court.

   c. Moving down the court that is wooden, the basketball player twists, leaps, and plays.

   d. Running, twisting, and leaping, the basketball player moved down the wooden court.

2.
   > He steals the ball.
   >
   > The ball is his opponent's.
   >
   > His stealing is quick.
   >
   > His stealing is with a deft movement.

   a. He, with a quick deft movement, steals the ball from his opponent.

   b. Quickly stealing the ball from his opponent, his stealing is with a deft movement.

   c. With a deft movement, he quickly steals the ball from his opponent.

   d. Stealing quickly his opponent's ball with a deft movement.

3.
   > He shoots.
   >
   > The ball rises.
   >
   > The rise is in an arc.
   >
   > The arc is perfect.
   >
   > The ball drops into the basket.
   >
   > The drop is smooth.

   a. He shoots, and the ball, rising in a perfect arc, drops smoothly into the basket.

   b. The drop into the basket is smooth as the ball rises in a perfect arc, and he shoots.

   c. He shoots, the ball rises, the ball drops, in a perfect arc, into the basket.

   d. He shoots smoothly, the ball rising perfectly in a dropping into the basket arc.

The Player (cont.)

4.
> James A. Naismith invented the game.
>
> He used a ball.
>
> He used a peach basket.
>
> The peach basket was wooden.
>
> The date was 1891.

 a. Using a ball and a peach basket that was wooden, James A. Naismith invented the game in 1891.

 b. Inventing the game in 1891, a ball and wooden peach basket James A. Naismith used.

 c. James A. Naismith, using a ball and a wooden peach basket, invented the game in 1891.

 d. In 1891, James A. Naismith used and invented a ball, wooden peach basket, and the game.

5.
> Players need to shoot the ball.
>
> Players need to pass the ball.
>
> Players need to dribble the ball.

 a. Players need to shoot the ball, pass the ball, and dribble the ball.

 b. Players need to shoot, pass, and dribble the ball.

 c. To shoot, to pass, and to dribble the ball is what players need.

 d. Players need to shoot and pass the ball, as well players need to dribble.

6.
> The crowd cheers.
>
> The crowd is excited.
>
> The cheering is wild.
>
> The crowd stands and claps.
>
> The clapping is for the player.

 a. Cheering wildly, the crowd stands and claps for the excited player.

 b. Standing, clapping, and cheering, the excited crowd is wild for the player.

 c. The crowd cheers and is excited and wild as it stands and claps for the player.

 d. The excited crowd, cheering wildly, stands and claps for the player.

Fun Fact! Did you know that Naismith combined the Native American game of lacrosse and the British game of soccer to make the inside game of basketball?

Igloos

Directions: Read the short sentences. Pick the answer choice that best combines the information in the short sentences. Your answer should be clear and grammatically correct.

1. | An igloo is a house.
    The house is made from blocks.
    The blocks are snow.
    Why doesn't an igloo melt inside?

   a. Why doesn't an igloo, a house made from blocks of snow, melt inside?
   b. An igloo is a house made from blocks of snow, and melt inside why doesn't it?
   c. Why doesn't a house made from blocks of snow melt inside an igloo?
   d. A house of blocks made from snow doesn't melt inside, and why is it an igloo?

2. | A lamp is lit inside the igloo.
    The lamp is burning.
    The lamp is hot.
    The lamp is lit after the blocks have been laid.

   a. A lamp that is hot and burning is lit after the blocks have been laid inside the igloo.
   b. After the blocks have been laid, a burning hot lamp is lit inside the igloo.
   c. Inside the igloo a burning hot lamp after the blocks have been laid is lit.
   d. The lamp is lit after the blocks have been lit, hot and burning, inside the igloo.

3. | The door is closed with a block of ice.
    The door is to the igloo.
    The lamp is burning.
    Everything is airtight.

   a. Everything is closed with a block of ice while the lamp is burning, and the igloo is airtight.
   b. Everything is burning and airtight while the igloo door is closed with a block of ice.
   c. While the lamp is burning, the door to the igloo is closed with a block of ice, and everything is airtight.
   d. Closed with a block of ice, the door to the igloo is airtight, and everything is burning.

Igloos *(cont.)*

4.
> Snow begins to melt.
> The snow does not drip.
> Instead the snow runs.
> The snow runs down the roof.
> The roof is domed.

  a. The roof is domed, and so the snow that begins to melt does not drip but instead runs down the sides.

  b. Instead of dripping, the snow that does not drip and begins to melt runs down the domed roof.

  c. Snow begins to melt, but instead of dripping, it runs down the domed roof.

  d. Running down the domed roof is snow that instead of dripping did not melt.

5.
> Something happens when the blocks of snow become sufficiently wet.
> The lamp is put out.
> The door is opened.
> The air rushes in.
> The air is outside.

  a. The lamp is put out, and the door is opened when the blocks of snow become wet, and the outside air rushes sufficiently in.

  b. When the blocks of snow become sufficiently wet, the lamp is put out, the door is opened, and the outside air rushes in.

  c. The outside air rushes in when the lamp is put out and when the door is opened the blocks of snow become sufficiently wet.

  d. Rushing in when the door is opened, the outside air puts out the lamp when the snow becomes sufficiently wet.

6.
> Something happens when the air rushes in!
> The air is cold.
> The snow house is fragile.
> The house turns into a dome.
> The dome is ice.
> The dome is strong.

  a. The dome of ice is turned into a strong snow house when the cold fragile air rushes in!

  b. The house is turned into a fragile dome of strong ice when the cold air rushes in!

  c. When the air rushes in, the air is cold, and the fragile snow house is turned into a dome of strong ice!

  d. When the cold air rushes in, the fragile snow house is turned into a strong dome of ice!

Fun fact! Did you know that a polar bear could crawl over the roof of an igloo without caving it in?

How Can It Be?

Directions: Read the short sentences. Pick the answer choice that best combines the information in the short sentences. Your answer should be clear and grammatically correct.

1.
> Joe was standing.
>
> The standing was calm.
>
> The standing was on a ladder.
>
> The stepladder was tall.
>
> Joe was my brother.
>
> Joe was little.

    a. Joe was standing on a tall ladder, and he was calm and little, but the ladder was tall.

    b. Standing calmly on a tall ladder, my little brother Joe was.

    c. Joe, my little brother, was standing calmly on a tall ladder.

    d. Joe, my little brother, on a ladder that was tall, was standing calmly.

2.
> The ladder reached.
>
> The reaching was over 30 feet.
>
> The ladder leaned against the building.
>
> The building was brick.

    a. Leaning against the building that was brick, the ladder reached 30 feet over.

    b. Leaning against the brick building, the ladder reached over 30 feet.

    c. The ladder, reaching over 30 feet, leaned, and it was against a building brick.

    d. The brick building reached the over 30-foot ladder leaning against it.

3.
> I told Joe to be careful.
>
> Joe just smiled.
>
> The smiling was wide.
>
> Joe just waved.

    a. I told Joe to be careful, but he just smiled widely and waved.

    b. Smiling widely, I told Joe to be careful and waved.

    c. The smile was wide, and Joe waved, but I told him to be careful.

    d. Telling Joe to be careful, he just widely smiled and waved.

How Can It Be? *(cont.)*

4.
> A gust of wind came.
>
> The gust was big.
>
> The gust caused Joe to teeter.
>
> The gust caused Joe to fall.

   a. A gust of wind that was big came, and the gust caused Joe to teeter and fall.

   b. Teetering and falling, the big gust of wind that came caused Joe.

   c. Causing Joe to teeter and causing Joe to fall, the big gust of wind came.

   d. A big gust of wind came, causing Joe to teeter and fall.

5.
> How could it be that Joe laughed?
>
> The laughing was merry.
>
> How could it be that Joe was not hurt?
>
> How could it be that Joe was not scared?

   a. Not hurt, or scared, merry Joe laughed, but how could it be?

   b. How could it be that Joe was not hurt, scared, and laughing merrily?

   c. How could it be that Joe laughed merrily and was not hurt or scared?

   d. The laughing merry, Joe was hurt, scared, not, but how could it be?

6.
> The ladder may have been tall.
>
> Joe was only standing.
>
> The standing was on a step.
>
> The step was the second.

   a. Only standing on the tall ladder, Joe may have been on the second step!

   b. The ladder may have been tall, but Joe was only standing on the second step!

   c. On the step that was second of the tall ladder, Joe may have been only standing!

   d. The ladder may have been tall, but standing on the second step only was Joe!

Fun fact! Did you know that a man went running in the rain, but not a hair on his head got wet? That's because the man was bald!

Safety Pin

Directions: Read the short sentences. Pick the answer choice that best combines the information in the short sentences. Your answer should be clear and grammatically correct.

1. | Walter Hunt owed money.
    | Walter Hunt was an inventor.
    | It was 1825.

    a. In 1825 Walter Hunt owed money to an inventor.

    b. Walter Hunt, an inventor, owed money, and he owed it in 1825.

    c. Walter Hunt, an inventor, owed money in 1825.

    d. In 1825 Walter Hunt owed money and inventor was he.

2. | Hunt owed a man money.
    | The man gave Hunt a wire.
    | The man told Hunt, "Invent something."

    a. The man to whom Hunt owed money gave Hunt a wire and said, "Invent something."

    b. The man Hunt owed money gave Hunt a wire, and Hunt said, "Invent something."

    c. "Invent something," the man who owed Hunt money and gave a wire to Hunt told him.

    d. Hunt was told, "Invent something," by a man owing him money and who gave him a wire.

3. | Hunt would give the man his invention.
    | The invention would be given instead of cash.

    a. Hunt would give the man his invention, and the invention giving would be instead of cash.

    b. Hunt would give the man his invention instead of cash.

    c. The invention would be given instead of cash, and the man would get Hunt's invention.

    d. Hunt would give the man his cash instead of his invention.

Safety Pin *(cont.)*

4. | Hunt fiddled with the wire.
Hunt fiddled for over three hours.
Hunt came up with the safety pin.

   a. Hunt fiddled with the wire for over three hours, so Hunt came up with the safety pin.
   b. Hunt came up with the wire after Hunt fiddled for over three hours with the safety pin.
   c. After coming up with the safety pin, Hunt fiddled for three hours.
   d. After fiddling with the wire for over three hours, Hunt came up with the safety pin.

5. | Pins were invented.
They were invented long ago.
Hunt improved an idea.
The idea was old.

   a. Pins were invented long ago, so Hunt improved an old idea that was invented long ago.
   b. Pins were invented long ago, but what Hunt did was improve an old idea.
   c. Hunt improved an idea that was old because pins were an idea invented long ago.
   d. Long ago an idea was invented, and Hunt improved the old pins.

6. | The pin Hunt made was stronger.
The pin Hunt made was springier.
The pin Hunt made was safer.

   a. Hunt's pin was stronger, springier, and safer.
   b. The pin Hunt made was stronger, springier, and safer, too.
   c. Hunt's pin was stronger and springier and safer.
   d. The pin Hunt made was stronger, springier, and was safer.

Fun Fact! Did you know that while Hunt may have paid his debt, the man to whom Hunt gave his invention made a fortune?

What Tim Needed

Directions: Read the short sentences. Pick the answer choice that best combines the information in the short sentences. Your answer should be clear and grammatically correct.

1. | Tim rose from his bed.
   | The rising was sleepy.
   | The bed was warm.
   | Tim threw off his blankets.
   | The blankets are heavy.

   a. Tim threw off his heavy blankets sleepily and rose from his warm bed.

   b. Throwing off his heavy blankets, Tim rose sleepily from his warm bed.

   c. Rising from his bed that was warm, Tim sleepily threw off his heavy blankets.

   d. Rising sleepily from his bed, Tim threw off his blankets that were heavy.

2. | Tim is rushing to get ready for school.
   | Tim dressed.
   | Tim ate.
   | Tim brushed his teeth.

   a. Tim is rushing to get ready for school, and Tim dressed and ate and brushed his teeth.

   b. Rushing to get ready for school, Tim dressed, ate, and brushed his teeth.

   c. Dressing, eating, and brushing his teeth, Tim is rushing to get ready for school.

   d. Tim, dressed, ate, and brushed his teeth, is rushing to get ready for school.

3. | Tim went to a room.
   | The room was his brother's.
   | Tim woke his brother up.

   a. Tim went to a room; the room was his brother's, and Tim woke his brother up.

   b. Waking his brother up, Tim went to a room that was his brother's.

   c. Tim went to his brother's room and woke him up.

   d. He woke him up, and Tim went to her brother's room.

What Tim Needed *(cont.)*

4.
> Willie was his brother.
>
> Willie cried.
>
> The crying was with anger.
>
> The cry was, "Let me be!"

    a. Willie was his brother, and he in anger cried, "Let me be!"

    b. Crying angrily "Let me be!" Willie was his brother.

    c. Willie, his brother, cried angrily, "Let me be!"

    d. "Let me be!" his angry brother Willie cried.

5.
> Willie was older.
>
> Willie was wiser.
>
> Willie reminded Tim that he could not be late for school.
>
> He could not be late, as it was Saturday.

    a. Willie, older and wiser, reminded Tim that, as it was Saturday, he could not be late for school.

    b. As it was Saturday, Tim was reminded by Willie, older and wiser, that he could not be late for school.

    c. He could not be late for school, Tim was reminded by Willie Saturday, as he was older and wiser.

    d. Older and wiser Willie could not be late for school, as it was Saturday, Tim was reminded.

6.
> Willie looked at Tim.
>
> Willie's eyes twinkled.
>
> Willie said, "You need a calendar."

    a. "You need a calendar," Willie's eyes twinkled and looked at Tim.

    b. Looking at Tim, "You need a calendar," Willie, eyes twinkling, said.

    c. Saying, "You need a calendar," Willie looked, eyes twinkling.

    d. Willie, eyes twinkling, looked at Tim and said, "You need a calendar."

Fun Fact! Did you know that a solar year is based on the sun cycle, while a lunar year is based on the moon cycle? A solar year is 365 days, 5 hours, 48 minutes, and 46 seconds long. A lunar year is 354 days, 8 hours, and 48 minutes long.

Coast Guard Pilot

Directions: Read the short sentences. Pick the answer choice that best combines the information in the short sentences. Your answer should be clear and grammatically correct.

1.
> Ken Tan is my uncle.
>
> Ken Tan is a Coast Guard pilot.
>
> Ken Tan is stationed in Alaska.

    a. Ken Tan, my uncle, is a Coast Guard pilot stationed in Alaska.

    b. My uncle stationed in Alaska, a Coast Guard pilot, Ken Tan.

    c. Stationed in Alaska is Ken Tan, my Coast Guard uncle pilot.

    d. Ken Tan is my uncle stationed in Alaska, a Coast Guard pilot.

2.
> Ken flies his helicopter.
>
> He flies into the night.
>
> The night is dark.
>
> The night is cold.
>
> He flies when people need help.

    a. Ken flies when people need help his helicopter into the cold, dark night.

    b. Into the night that is cold and dark, Ken flies when people need his helicopter help.

    c. Flying his helicopter into the cold and dark night when people need help is Ken.

    d. When people need help, Ken flies his helicopter into the cold, dark night.

3.
> The sea waves were high.
>
> The waves were over 100 feet (30.48 meters).
>
> The waves were wild.
>
> The waves were in one storm.
>
> The storm was fierce.

    a. In one fierce storm, the wild sea waves were over 100 feet (30.48 meters) high.

    b. The high and over 100 feet (30.48 meters) sea waves were in one wild, fierce storm.

    c. The sea waves were high, wild, and over 100 feet (30.48 meters), and one storm was fierce.

    d. In one storm that was fierce, the wild waves of the sea were over 100 feet high (30.48 meters).

Coast Guard Pilot *(cont.)*

4.
> Ken kept the helicopter level.
> It was level despite the wind.
> The wind was in gusts.
> The basket was dropped.

   a. Ken, dropping the basket, kept the helicopter level despite the wind that came in gusts.

   b. Despite keeping the helicopter level, Ken dropped the basket in the gusts of wind.

   c. Keeping the helicopter level, the wind gusting despite, Ken dropped the basket.

   d. Despite the gusts of wind, Ken kept the helicopter level, and the basket was dropped.

5.
> Rescue swimmers jumped.
> The jumping was into the water.
> The water was churning.
> The swimmers were in wetsuits.
> The swimmers were in flippers.

   a. Into the churning water in wetsuits and flippers jumped rescue swimmers.

   b. Rescue swimmers, in wetsuits and flippers, jumped into the churning water.

   c. Rescue swimmers jumped into the water that was churning, and the swimmers were wetsuits and flippers.

   d. Into wetsuits, flippers, and the churning water, rescue swimmers jumped.

6.
> Ken says a rescue is a team effort.
> The effort is with a pilot.
> The effort is with rescue swimmers.
> The effort is with a flight mechanic.
> They all work as one.

   a. All working as one, Ken says the pilot, rescue swimmers, and flight mechanic are a rescue team effort.

   b. Ken says a rescue is a team effort, and the pilot, rescue swimmers, and flight mechanic, they all work as one.

   c. Ken says a rescue is a team effort, with the pilot, rescue swimmers, and flight mechanic all working as one.

   d. A pilot, rescue swimmers, flight mechanic, and Ken together say a rescue is an as one team effort.

Fun Fact! Did you know that an old Coast Guard saying is, "You have to go out, but you don't necessarily have to come back"?

How the People Got Salt, a Cochiti Myth

Directions: Read the short sentences. Pick the answer choice that best combines the information in the short sentences. Your answer should be clear and grammatically correct.

1.
   Salt Woman was old.

   Salt Woman was poor.

   Her grandson was poor.

   People were too busy cooking to feed them.

   The cooking was for a feast.

   a. Cooking for a feast, old Salt Woman and her grandson were too busy to feed people.

   b. Busy cooking for a feast, old Salt Woman and her poor grandson were not fed by people.

   c. Old Salt Woman and her grandson were poor, but people busy cooking for a feast fed them, too.

   d. Old Salt Woman and her grandson were poor, but people were too busy cooking for a feast to feed them.

2.
   Salt Woman was hungry.

   Salt Woman was upset.

   Salt Woman went to where all the children were playing.

   The children were little.

   a. Hungry and upset, Salt Woman went to where all the little children were playing.

   b. Upset, Salt Woman was hungry and went to where all the playing children were little.

   c. Salt Woman went to where all the little children were playing, hungry and upset.

   d. Salt Woman, hungry and upset, went to where all the children who were little were playing.

3.
   Salt Woman turned the children into jays.

   The jays were noisy.

   She turned them with her crystal.

   The crystal was magic.

   a. Salt Woman, with her crystal that was magic, turned the noisy jays into children.

   b. The children were turned into noisy jays by the magic crystal that was Salt Woman's.

   c. Salt Woman turned the children into noisy jays with her magic crystal.

   d. Turning the children into noisy jays, Salt Woman did with her magic crystal.

How the People Got Salt, a Cochiti Myth *(cont.)*

4.
> Salt Woman and her grandson traveled.
> The traveling was south.
> They met people.
> The people were kind.
> The people fed them well.

   a. Salt Woman and her grandson traveled, and south they met kind people who fed them well.

   b. Traveling south, Salt Woman and her grandson met kind people who fed them well.

   c. The kind people who fed them well were south where Salt Woman and her grandson traveled.

   d. The people who fed them well were kind, and Salt Woman and her grandson met them south traveling.

5.
> Salt Woman was thankful.
> Salt Woman left the people some of her flesh.
> The people were good.
> The flesh was salty.
> The flesh was to put in their food.

   a. Thankful, Salt Woman left the good people some of her salty flesh to put in their food.

   b. Salt Woman was thankful, and she left the good people some of her flesh to put in their food that was salty.

   c. Salt Woman left the thankful people some of her salty flesh to put in their good food.

   d. Salt Woman left the thankful good people some of her salty flesh to put in their food.

6.
> The people wanted more salt.
> The people listened to Salt Woman.
> Salt Woman told them where they could find salt.
> The salt was at Salt Lake.

   a. Listening to Salt Woman, the people wanted more salt where they could find it at Salt Lake.

   b. Salt Woman told the people where they could find more wanted salt at Salt Lake as they listened.

   c. The people wanted more salt, and Salt Woman listened to the people as she told them where they could find the salt that was at Salt Lake.

   d. Wanting more salt, the people listened to Salt Woman as she told them where they could find salt at Salt Lake.

Fun Fact! Did you know that the Cochiti are a Native American people from the southwestern United States?

Walking in Circles

Directions: Read the short sentences. Pick the answer choice that best combines the information in the short sentences. Your answer should be clear and grammatically correct.

1.
> One will end up walking in circles if blindfolded.
> One will end up walking in circles if stranded in fog.
> One will end up walking in circles if lost in a snowstorm.
> Why will one end up walking in circles?

    a. Why will one end up walking in circles if blinded or if stranded in fog or if lost in a snowstorm?

    b. One will end up walking in circles if blindfolded, stranded in fog, or lost in a snowstorm, and why?

    c. Why will one end up in circles if blindfolded, stranded in fog, or lost in a snowstorm walking?

    d. Why will one end up walking in circles if blindfolded, stranded in fog, or lost in a snowstorm?

2.
> The body is asymmetrical.
> The body is human.
> Asymmetrical means it is not balanced.
> The balance is between sides.
> The sides are left and right.
> The balance is not perfect.

    a. The body that is human is asymmetrical, meaning the right and left sides are not perfectly balanced.

    b. The human body is not in balance because it is asymmetrical, and the right side is not balanced with the perfect left.

    c. The human body is asymmetrical, meaning that the right and left sides are not perfectly balanced.

    d. Due to left and right sides not in perfect balance, the asymmetrical body is human.

3.
> There is an example.
> The example is with the heart.
> The heart is on our left side.
> The example is with the liver.
> The liver is on our right side.

    a. For example, the heart is on our left side, while the liver is on our right side.

    b. The heart, for example, is on our left side while, for example, the liver is on our right.

    c. For example, the heart and liver are on the right side and the left side.

    d. The example is the heart and the liver because they are on the left and right side.

Walking in Circles (cont.)

4.
> Our muscles differ from side to side.
>
> The sides are left to right.
>
> The muscles affect our gait.
>
> Gait means a way of walking or running.

   a. Our muscles differ from side to side, right and left, so our gait affects our walking or running way muscles.

   b. Gait means a way of walking or running, and it is affected by our muscles that differ from right to left side.

   c. Since our right to left have muscles that differ from side to side, our gait (the way we walk or run) is affected.

   d. Since our muscles differ from right side to left side, our gait (the way we walk or run) is affected.

5.
> Our body's structure controls our gait.
>
> Our muscles control our gait.
>
> The control is when we close our eyes.

   a. Control, when we close our eyes, of our body's structure, muscles, and gait.

   b. When we close our eyes, our body's structure and muscles control our gait.

   c. When we close our eyes, the control that is of our gait depends on our body and muscle structure.

   d. The control of our muscles and structure of our body is our gait when we close our eyes.

6.
> One side forces us to turn.
>
> The turn is in a direction.
>
> The direction is certain.
>
> We end up walking.
>
> The walk is in a circle.

   a. One side forces us to turn in a certain direction, and we end up walking in a circle.

   b. One side forces us to turn in a certain circle direction, and we end walking up.

   c. We end up walking, and one side forces us to in a certain direction circle turn.

   d. We turn in a circle direction when we walk, and one side forces us to certainly turn.

Fun Fact! Did you know that controlled tests have shown that blindfolded drivers will begin to drive off a straight road in about 20 seconds?

First and New

Directions: Read the short sentences. Fill in the answer choice that best combines the information in the short sentences. Your answer should be clear and grammatically correct.

1.
> My brother always sees things first.
>
> My brother is older.
>
> My brother is Leon.

(a) My brother is Leon, and he always sees things first, and he is older.

(b) Leon, my older brother, always sees things first.

(c) Older and first, my brother Leon always sees things.

(d) My brother Leon always sees older things first.

2.
> One day I had an idea.
>
> The day was in the spring.
>
> The idea was big.
>
> I asked a farmer for a thing.
>
> The thing was small.

(a) One big spring day I had an idea, but I asked a farmer for a small thing.

(b) I asked a big farmer for a small thing one day in the spring when I had an idea.

(c) One spring day I had a big idea, and I asked a farmer for a small thing.

(d) I had a big idea, and I asked the farmer a small thing for spring one day.

3.
> The farmer said, "Keep it warm."
>
> The farmer was old.
>
> The farmer handed me something.
>
> The thing was small.
>
> The thing was white.
>
> The thing was smooth.

(a) "Keep it warm," handing me something small, white, and smooth, said the old farmer.

(b) The farmer said warmly, "Keep it," handing me something small, white, and smooth.

(c) Handing me it, the old farmer said, "Keep the small, white, smooth thing warm."

(d) "Keep it warm," the old farmer said, handing me something small, white, and smooth.

First and New (cont.)

4.
> Leon laughed.
> The laugh was hearty.
> Leon grinned.
> The grin was at me.
> Leon said, "I've seen it before."
> Leon said, "Show me something new."

(a) Laughing heartily, Leon grinned at me and said, "I've seen it before; show me something new."

(b) "I've seen it before; show me something new," Leon said at me when he heartily laughed and grinned.

(c) Laughing and grinning heartily, Leon said at me, "I've seen it before," and, "Show me something new."

(d) "I've seen it before," and "Show me something new," are what Leon said laughing heartily and grinned at me.

5.
> A chick pecked its way out of the egg.
> The chick was yellow.
> The chick was downy.
> When the chick pecked, I saw it first.

(a) First, I saw a yellow, downy chick peck its way out of the egg.

(b) When a yellow, downy chick pecked its way out of the egg, I saw it first.

(c) Yellow and downy, I saw a chick first when it pecked its way out of the egg.

(d) The yellow and downy chick pecked its way out first of the egg when I saw it.

6.
> Leon said, "You saw it first."
> Leon said, "And it's new."
> Leon looked at the chick.
> Leon looked in wonder.
> The chick was little.

(a) Leon, looking, said in wonder, "The little chick is new, and you saw it first."

(b) Looking at the little chick and looking in wonder, Leon said, "You saw it first, and it's new."

(c) "You saw it first," said Leon in wonder, looking at the little chick, "And it's new."

(d) "You saw it first, and it's new," said Leon, looking at the little chick in wonder.

Fun Fact! Did you know that chicks have an "egg tooth" to help them peck their way out of eggs? The "tooth" is at the top tip of its beak, and it falls off or wears away soon after the chick hatches.

Island Talk

Directions: Read the short sentences. Fill in the answer choice that best combines the information in the short sentences. Your answer should be clear and grammatically correct.

1.

> Bruce sits at his desk.
>
> Bruce travels the world at his desk.
>
> The desk is for work.
>
> Bruce is a radio operator.

(a) Bruce, a radio operator, works traveling the world at his desk sitting.

(b) Sitting at his work desk, Bruce is a traveling world radio operator.

(c) Bruce sits at his desk that is for work and travels the world with his radio operator.

(d) A radio operator, Bruce sits at his work desk and travels the world.

2.

> Bruce has talked to people.
>
> The talk is with Bruce's radio.
>
> The people are on over 476 islands.
>
> The islands are all around the world.

(a) Bruce has talked to over 476 islands all around the world with people on them with his radio.

(b) Talking to radio people, Bruce has been to over 476 islands all around the world.

(c) With his radio, Bruce has talked to people on over 476 islands all around the world.

(d) Talking over Bruce's radio, people all around the world on 476 islands have talked.

3.

> Bruce's radio has a range.
>
> It is affected by weather conditions.
>
> It is affected by sunspots.
>
> It is affected even by solar flares.

(a) Bruce's range of the radio is affected by weather conditions, sunspots, and even solar flares.

(b) Weather conditions, sunspots, and even solar flares affect Bruce's radio range.

(c) Weather conditions, and sunspots, as well as solar flares even affect Bruce's radio range.

(d) Bruce's affected radio range is even weather conditions, sunspots, and solar flares.

Island Talk *(cont.)*

4.

> Bruce once talked to a man.
>
> The man was on Aves Island.
>
> Aves Island is a rock.
>
> The rock is tiny.
>
> The rock is off the coast of Venezuela.
>
> The rock is in the Atlantic Ocean.

(a) Bruce once talked to a man on Aves Island, a tiny rock off the coast of Venezuela in the Atlantic Ocean.

(b) On a tiny rock off the coast of Venezuela named Aves Island, Bruce once talked to a man in the Atlantic Ocean.

(c) Bruce, on tiny rock Aves Island, once talked off the coast of Venezuela in the Atlantic Ocean.

(d) Aves Island, in the Atlantic Ocean, is off the coast of Venezuela where Bruce once talked to a man.

5.

> Bruce was warm.
>
> Bruce talked to a scientist.
>
> The scientist was on an island.
>
> The scientist was cold!
>
> The island was near Antarctica.

(a) While warm, Bruce talked to a cold scientist near Antarctica's island!

(b) Antarctica's cold island was where Bruce talked to a scientist when he was warm!

(c) Bruce was warm, but the scientist he talked to on an island near Antarctica was cold!

(d) Bruce was warm, but the scientist was cold when Bruce talked to the island near Antarctica!

6.

> Bruce talked on Saturday.
>
> Bruce talked to a boy.
>
> The boy was on an island.
>
> It was already Sunday on the island!

(a) Bruce talked to a boy on Sunday on an island one Saturday!

(b) One Saturday, Bruce talked to a boy on an island where it was already Sunday!

(c) One Sunday on an island Bruce talked to a boy already on Saturday!

(d) Bruce talked on Saturday to a boy on an island where it was already Sunday on the island!

Fun Fact! **Did you know that in order to get his radio license, Bruce had to learn Morse code?**

Practice Answer Sheet

This sheet may be reproduced and used with the sentence combining questions. Each box can be used with one page. Using the answer sheets with the sentence combining exercises gives extra practice in test preparation.

The Yo-Yo	Should We Tell?	Swimming in Antarctica
1. (a) (b) (c) (d)	1. (a) (b) (c) (d)	1. (a) (b) (c) (d)
2. (a) (b) (c) (d)	2. (a) (b) (c) (d)	2. (a) (b) (c) (d)
3. (a) (b) (c) (d)	3. (a) (b) (c) (d)	3. (a) (b) (c) (d)
4. (a) (b) (c) (d)	4. (a) (b) (c) (d)	4. (a) (b) (c) (d)
5. (a) (b) (c) (d)	5. (a) (b) (c) (d)	5. (a) (b) (c) (d)
6. (a) (b) (c) (d)	6. (a) (b) (c) (d)	6. (a) (b) (c) (d)

My Dog Hercules	Where in the World?	Riddles
1. (a) (b) (c) (d)	1. (a) (b) (c) (d)	1. (a) (b) (c) (d)
2. (a) (b) (c) (d)	2. (a) (b) (c) (d)	2. (a) (b) (c) (d)
3. (a) (b) (c) (d)	3. (a) (b) (c) (d)	3. (a) (b) (c) (d)
4. (a) (b) (c) (d)	4. (a) (b) (c) (d)	4. (a) (b) (c) (d)
5. (a) (b) (c) (d)	5. (a) (b) (c) (d)	5. (a) (b) (c) (d)
6. (a) (b) (c) (d)	6. (a) (b) (c) (d)	6. (a) (b) (c) (d)

The Zebra	The Scary Ride	Albert José Jones
1. (a) (b) (c) (d)	1. (a) (b) (c) (d)	1. (a) (b) (c) (d)
2. (a) (b) (c) (d)	2. (a) (b) (c) (d)	2. (a) (b) (c) (d)
3. (a) (b) (c) (d)	3. (a) (b) (c) (d)	3. (a) (b) (c) (d)
4. (a) (b) (c) (d)	4. (a) (b) (c) (d)	4. (a) (b) (c) (d)
5. (a) (b) (c) (d)	5. (a) (b) (c) (d)	5. (a) (b) (c) (d)
6. (a) (b) (c) (d)	6. (a) (b) (c) (d)	6. (a) (b) (c) (d)

Practice Answer Sheet *(cont.)*

The Wish

1. (a) (b) (c) (d)
2. (a) (b) (c) (d)
3. (a) (b) (c) (d)
4. (a) (b) (c) (d)
5. (a) (b) (c) (d)
6. (a) (b) (c) (d)

The Magic School Bus

1. (a) (b) (c) (d)
2. (a) (b) (c) (d)
3. (a) (b) (c) (d)
4. (a) (b) (c) (d)
5. (a) (b) (c) (d)
6. (a) (b) (c) (d)

The Player

1. (a) (b) (c) (d)
2. (a) (b) (c) (d)
3. (a) (b) (c) (d)
4. (a) (b) (c) (d)
5. (a) (b) (c) (d)
6. (a) (b) (c) (d)

Igloos

1. (a) (b) (c) (d)
2. (a) (b) (c) (d)
3. (a) (b) (c) (d)
4. (a) (b) (c) (d)
5. (a) (b) (c) (d)
6. (a) (b) (c) (d)

How Can It Be?

1. (a) (b) (c) (d)
2. (a) (b) (c) (d)
3. (a) (b) (c) (d)
4. (a) (b) (c) (d)
5. (a) (b) (c) (d)
6. (a) (b) (c) (d)

Safety Pin

1. (a) (b) (c) (d)
2. (a) (b) (c) (d)
3. (a) (b) (c) (d)
4. (a) (b) (c) (d)
5. (a) (b) (c) (d)
6. (a) (b) (c) (d)

What Tim Needed

1. (a) (b) (c) (d)
2. (a) (b) (c) (d)
3. (a) (b) (c) (d)
4. (a) (b) (c) (d)
5. (a) (b) (c) (d)
6. (a) (b) (c) (d)

Coast Guard Pilot

1. (a) (b) (c) (d)
2. (a) (b) (c) (d)
3. (a) (b) (c) (d)
4. (a) (b) (c) (d)
5. (a) (b) (c) (d)
6. (a) (b) (c) (d)

How the People Got Salt, a Cochiti Myth

1. (a) (b) (c) (d)
2. (a) (b) (c) (d)
3. (a) (b) (c) (d)
4. (a) (b) (c) (d)
5. (a) (b) (c) (d)
6. (a) (b) (c) (d)

Walking in Circles

1. (a) (b) (c) (d)
2. (a) (b) (c) (d)
3. (a) (b) (c) (d)
4. (a) (b) (c) (d)
5. (a) (b) (c) (d)
6. (a) (b) (c) (d)

Answer Key

The Yo-Yo
1. A
2. C
3. D
4. B
5. B
6. C

Should We Tell?
1. B
2. D
3. A
4. A
5. B
6. C

Swimming in Antarctica
1. B
2. D
3. C
4. A
5. A
6. C

My Dog Hercules
1. B
2. D
3. B
4. A
5. C
6. D

Where in the World?
1. D
2. A
3. B
4. C
5. D
6. A

Riddles
1. D
2. D

3. B
4. A
5. C
6. A

The Zebra
1. D
2. A
3. D
4. B
5. C
6. C

The Scary Ride
1. B
2. B
3. A
4. B
5. A
6. C

Albert José Jones
1. B
2. C
3. C
4. D
5. A
6. D

The Wish
1. C
2. B
3. D
4. A
5. C
6. B

The Magic School Bus
1. C
2. C
3. A

4. B
5. D
6. B

The Player
1. D
2. C
3. A
4. C
5. B
6. D

Igloos
1. A
2. B
3. C
4. C
5. B
6. D

How Can It Be?
1. C
2. B
3. A
4. D
5. C
6. B

Safety Pin
1. C
2. A
3. B
4. D
5. B
6. A

What Tim Needed
1. B
2. B
3. C
4. C
5. A
6. D

Coast Guard Pilot
1. A
2. D
3. A
4. D
5. B
6. C

How the People Got Salt, a Cochiti Myth
1. D
2. A
3. C
4. B
5. A
6. D

Walking in Circles
1. D
2. C
3. A
4. D
5. B
6. A

First and New
1. B
2. C
3. D
4. A
5. B
6. D

Island Talk
1. D
2. C
3. B
4. A
5. C
6. B